Don't
It Will Ruin *Everything*

Bern Callahan

Edited: Kathleen Doyle
Cartoons: Claudio DeMarco

Don't Wake Up! It Will Ruin Everything *offers insights about mindfulness practice* and an ironic commentary on several attitudes that are obstacles to waking up through mindfulness practice.

Don't Wake Up! It Will Ruin Everything's *insights on mindfulness appear in italic font.*

The commentary on attitudes that get in the way of mindfulness appears in plain print.

For my friends and readers
who helped along the way
For Evan and Kaylen
thanks for your encouragement
For Margaret, with a loving bow

A free audio copy of *Don't Wake Up!* is available on the book's FaceBook page. You can find *Don't Wake Up!* at https://www.facebook.com/DontWakeUp Book

Don't Wake Up

Waking up ruins everything. We've heard all kinds of wonderful tales about enlightenment, the great awakening of heart and mind. They're dangerous.

You could lose everything when you wake up.

- Your cherished self-identity can melt away.
- Your carefully constructed story about your accomplishments and about why you are right and others are wrong will be undercut.
- Your core beliefs about how the world works will be challenged.

Why would we want to wake up when we are perfectly comfortable right now? OK, perfectly comfortable might be an overstatement. Comfortable enough. Your life is working, isn't it? Your relationships are acceptable, aren't they? Your worldview explains it all in a way that enhances your life, doesn't it? Why risk all this by waking up?

The so-called dream we're having is perfectly good. It's not some version of *Friday The 13th, Nightmare On Elm Street,* or *The Walking Dead,* is it? No! In your dream you get up from the same bed each day, with the same sleeping partner, or alone, as usual. You brush your teeth at the same sink each day, have the same job, the same ambitions, the same conflicts, the same opinions, the same lover(s), the same enemies, the same conversations, the same frustrations, the same minor pleasures, and occasionally, the same orgasms. Why change any of that?

This book will help you stay in your chosen dream. It will help insulate you from recognizing that everything you think is really just your story about life. It will protect you from seeing that everything eventually changes. It will allow you to continue to believe that you and whoever, or whatever, you love is permanent and unchanging. At the same time, it will allow you to entertain the fantasy that whoever or whatever you dislike can be changed or eliminated.

This book is a satirical argument for solidity, permanence, and the true "self."

This book will also help you defend yourself against becoming mindful or meditating. If you want to be happy, these activities are dangerous and a complete waste of your time. If you engage with mindfulness or meditation, you might even find yourself questioning your whole view of happiness. It's better to never start, or at least to stop before you are hurt.

So, here it is: my best advice after 40 years of spiritual seeking, meditating, and studying philosophy. Don't wake up! It's dangerous and can ruin everything.

Here's a short description of the chapters in this book and what you will learn:

- **The Story:** You Don't Want To Know About The Story. Protect yourself from recognizing that everything is a story and the potential danger this insight poses.

- **Impermanence:** You Don't Want To Know That Everything Changes. Protect yourself from an insight that threatens your fixed ideas and opinions.

- **Result:** You' Don't Want To Know That Related Effect Always Follows Action. Protect yourself from an understanding of how karma works. It's easier and better to think that it's the other guy's credit or fault.

- **Me:** You Don't Want To Know About Non-Self. Protect yourself from understanding that identity is a made-up-idea, constantly changing and fickle. There's nowhere to hang your hat.

- **Openness:** You Definitely Don't Want To Know About Openness. Protect yourself from understanding Emptiness. It's way better to think that things are real. It's more comforting, easier to understand, and generally matches our dreams and illusions.

- **Awake Mind:** You Definitely Don't Want To Know About The Potential For Awake Mind. Protect yourself from having an open and dynamic mind and all the bother of having to re-examine the contents of your thoughts.

- **Open Heart:** You Most Definitely Don't Want To Experience An Open Heart. Protect yourself from feeling too much. Feelings are messy. It's far better when they are scripted and predictable. Being open hearted threatens all of the benefits of predictable emotions and life-scripts.

- **Showing Up:** You Absolutely Don't Want To Have To Show Up. Protect yourself from the demands to be present, to show up, and to do something useful. It's so much less scary, so much better to stay in the dream and think that your presence doesn't matter, can't effect any meaningful change, or isn't needed.

- **Strategies For Staying Asleep**: Ten Actions That Will Satisfy Your Hunger To Remain Oblivious. Protect yourself against those activities and ways of being that threaten your peaceful, dream-filled sleep.

- **Afterword:** The Choice To Sleep Or To Wake Up.

Recognizing how our stories, our choices, desires, and assumptions keep us asleep allows us to choose to wake up or to stay in the dream.

The Story

Your truth is predictable, logical, and provable. Your friends, family, neighbors, and colleagues, believe it. Your story is comfortable for members of your church, synagogue, mosque, temple, and Google group.

Want to hear an example of a comfortable story that we all want to believe? Here's one: I have a "self." That "self" is something that I will always have. In fact, that "self" is permanent and continues after I die. No sane person denies death. However, we tell ourselves stories about heaven and hell and the afterlife, and reincarnation. They're all stories about the continuing self. All of these stories depend upon a "self." If there isn't a "self," then stories about what happens to it after death would make absolutely no sense.

No one has ever found this "self." Many philosophers and religious thinkers have searched without finding it. This "self" has no location. I can't say it's in my head without ignoring my heart. I can't say it's just a feeling in my gut. It's hard, almost impossible, to pin it down.

It's also impossible to say what shape this "self" is. Is it square, round, flat, spherical, shaped like a cube or barbell, or what? If you search for the shape, you won't find it beyond something in your imagination. If you do find it, then a skilled surgeon should be able to go in and remove it. In some near science fiction future, maybe we could merge the "self" with artificial life or intelligence and achieve immortality. However, that scenario depends on the existence of a real, palpable, findable self.

Clever thinkers have said that the "self" has no physical existence. We can't find it because it isn't physical. It's spiritual or mental or emotional. That's all OK. But here's the question. What, if any, difference is there between this spiritual self we assume and the Easter Bunny? Or between the mental self we imagine and the Tooth Fairy? Or between the emotional self we desire and any fantasy?

In truth, these arguments for a spiritual, mental, or emotional "self" allow us to continue to believe in the story of a self without suffering the burden of having to prove that one exists. When all else fails, we can say, "People have always thought this" or "God told us this is how it is." We can't actually prove it ourselves, but we have it on good authority.

Once we've carefully established that you indeed have a "self," then we need a story. Stuff happened and you were (choose one) right or wrong. Let's keep it simple. You were right. Your point of view was the most correct. Your understanding of history, current events, politics, and philosophy is the most accurate. People should agree with you. When they don't, they are to some degree wrong. If you're polite, they're mistaken. If you're not polite, they're dumb. Either way, you get to keep your story.

Recently I had a phone conversation with my twin brother. I have an identical twin who has a surprisingly different story than I do. He reminded me of something stupid that I did and said when we were still teenagers. That was more than four decades ago.

My instinct was to correct him. I wanted to remind him of all the parts of the story he was leaving out. His story couldn't be correct. I held my tongue and kept those thoughts to myself. We had a satisfying conversation. At least that's my story. We promised to talk again soon.

After that phone call, I questioned my own story. What if my memory wasn't accurate? What did it mean that I had not bothered to remember the incident my twin reminded me of? Why was that part of his story and not part of mine? Why were important parts of my story missing from his memory? We shared everything once, even conception. How could we remember things so differently?

We live in a fascinating time when a super abundance of information is available to almost everyone. At the same time, I am intimately aware of my own "self" and my story. There's so much to explore that I don't know much about. I know almost nothing about the ice shelves of Antarctica, or the cultural history of the Amazon tribes, or about Islam. I know lots about Christianity and Buddhism. However, I know that information from within two very specific filters.

I know Christianity from within Catholicism and I know Buddhism from within Tibetan Buddhism. I don't know what it feels like to be a Protestant, or to practice Pure Land Japanese Buddhism. I'm not familiar with Evangelical thinkers or with the Pali Canon of the Buddhist traditions of South Asia. It is so tempting to think that I know something even while I don't know everything.

When I'm asked my opinion, I have one automatically. I don't stop very often to look and see whether my opinion is well grounded in facts or based in experience. I just have one. It's easier that way.

Of course, I can search the Internet and find support for my opinion. It's out there somewhere. I just have to define my search. Contrary opinions and stories are either mistaken or stupid. I can pass those by. Why would I want to be curious about someone else's story if it's different from mine? Why would I want to open my story up to the possibilities of being challenged or changed? I like my story the way it is. So I'm sticking with it no matter what.

One dangerous truth that is understood upon awakening is that everything is a story.

The "self" that we all experience is a story made up to offer continuity to the demonstrable temporariness of everything.

I felt happy this morning, sad this afternoon, and in love tonight. Where did the happiness or sadness go? I used to identify with and love the busyness of the city. Now I love the quiet of the country. Where did my love for busyness go?

Waking up shows us that our loves, preferences, thoughts, and even our memories are constantly changing. They are a story we tell ourselves. We tell the same story over and over again to cement it within our awareness and make it real. We've been telling the story for so long that we've forgotten that we're even telling a story. We think the story is real.

Once you see that you're telling a story, you won't be able to regard it with the same seriousness ever again. You'll be forced to ask questions like "Is this the best story?" "Is this the story I want to be in?" "Is this story worth continuing?" "Do I want to change how this story ends?"

Waking up kills a good story. If you like how your life is right now, avoid recognizing that you're telling a story for as long as possible.

Impermanence

If you want to stay asleep, definitely hold onto the dream that everything you love stays the same and everything you hate, moderately dislike, or just plain don't care about, will also always stay the same. You are the same person you remember from your first day at school.

Nothing essential about you has changed. You have the same name. Your parents are still your parents. Your attendance record and grade school report cards are fixed for all times as a permanent record. In fact, there's nothing essential about you that has changed from even before that fateful first day at school. You're still the younger brother, the funny shy one, who smiles a lot.

Sure, you grow and add new memories. This is like a tree growing. You might have a thicker trunk, more leaves, and taller limbs, but you're the same tree as that little sapling. It's like there is more of you rather than less of you. Nothing is forgotten or left behind.

The same thing is true of your loved ones. Your mom and dad will always be who you remember them being. Even when they descend into old age and its frailties, they are still there to support you as their child. It doesn't matter that they're in their late 80's and you're 53. Nothing changes.

That woman or man you fell in love with is the same person she or he has always been, too. She's the young woman you met at the dance or bar or church event or whatever. She's the same as she was when she wore that summer dress and you danced all night. It doesn't matter that she's now the mother of your three children and is no longer 19. She's the same as she's always been, maybe more but the same. That man you met: handsome, funny, maybe a little outrageous, he's the same, too. He's still ambitious and curious even though he hasn't shown much of that lately. It's all there, under the surface of his mid-forties funk. It doesn't matter that his career appears stalled in mid-management and that he isn't that interested in making love with you anymore. He's still the same. He has to be.

And your kids, they never change. They're still sweet, happy, uncomplicated, and fun. It doesn't matter that Sally now has two little ones of her own and has divorced her husband. It doesn't change anything that Bill came out two years ago as gay. Nothing changes. They're the same as they always were and you love them for it.

Politics never change. Your opinion hasn't had any significant alterations since the late 1990's when you changed your mind about those computer things. Facts aren't important and reasoning is even less important than that. You know what you feel in your gut and nothing's changing that.

Most of all, the physical world never changes. That's why all this climate change stuff is a grand hoax perpetrated by manipulative know-it-alls on the unsuspecting. The house you grew up in is still in the same suburb you left in the early 1990's. Summers have always been hot. Hurricanes and landslides and droughts and forest fires have always occurred. There's nothing new going on even if every one of the last three years has each successively been the hottest year on record. Maybe our record keeping has improved, but the physical world hasn't changed one little bit.

Same As It Ever Was.

Another dangerous truth that is understood upon awakening is that everything changes.

If we look carefully, we can witness these changes taking place all the time. Just look at the second hand of your clock or watch. Time is constantly changing. The seeds in your garden grow, flower, fruit, and then fade back in autumn. You are not the same person you always were. You were once a little girl or boy. Now you are a grown woman or man with your loves and passions and your fears and hopes. Sometime, if you are lucky, you will become an old woman or old man with your memories, accumulated wisdom and scars of the heart. We all know the wise old woman isn't the little girl even if we can see a connection between the two. Grandpop is not the high school running back he used to be. It's just easier to regard them as the same.

If things can change, then life isn't just happening to you. You are part of the flow and drama of this dance. Your role, your impact, your importance, your happiness or unhappiness can change. That's a lot of self-responsibility. Who wants that?

Change will break your heart wide open. The sweet teeter-totter of life doesn't guarantee anything because it can change in the blink of an eye. Lovers become enemies. Happily married spouses see each other only when accompanied by their divorce lawyers. Your children grow up and leave home. Maybe they take the time to talk with you. Maybe they don't.

Allies and friends become enemies. Leaders change and the new leaders say stupid things that offend friends who have been collectively cultivated over decades or centuries. Revolutions overturn the respected order and threaten the hold on power by the rich privileged few.

Revolutions are messy. I remember being quite glad when President Ronald Reagan redefined the American revolution of 1776 as *The War of Independence*. With that name switch, the implied deep changes of revolution were overwritten by a sanitized independence from an unidentified something. No longer "free at last," we were all "safe at last."

Waking up is a revolution that kills the sense of security that comes from believing that things will always be this way. If you are happy with how things are right now, then do your best to deny or ignore change as long as you can.

Result

It's much easier to deal with life if we are unburdened by the idea of result being related to prior action. Things just happen the way they were designed to happen. There's no connection between what was done or happened before with what is happening now.

Some people are born lucky. If you are one of the lucky ones, you can celebrate. If you are not one of the lucky ones, it's not your fault. You were born this way.

- A young black man isn't angry because he recognizes that he's many, many times more likely to be killed by the police or arrested than a white kid from the suburbs. He's just angry because he's black.
- Steve Job's famous obsession with quality and design had nothing to do with his success. Jobs was just fortunate to be at the right place at the right time and got lucky with the Mac, then lucky again with the iPhone, and then lucky a

third time with the iPad. It had nothing to do with effort or persistence.

- Poverty, crime, and disease have nothing to do with the conditions that people live in. It's like a garden. There are good seeds and bad seeds. The condition of the soil or the care given to plants after planting has little to zero effect.

- Spiritual awakening has nothing to do with effort. I believe in Faith Alone, Instant Enlightenment, the Wizard of Oz, Burning Bush awakenings. It has nothing to do with training the heart, apprenticing with a master, or opening the mind. It just happens. God lays it on you and there it is.

Life is also easier if we allow ourselves to believe that the same actions produce different results for different people.

Take that person in the gym, the one with the sculpted physique who I look at out of the corner of my eye. His fitness has nothing to do with the hours he spends at the gym or his obsession with eating a lean diet. No, it's the special machine he uses to exercise. This is proven every time I see the advertisement for Abmaster or Thigh-Buster or Butt-Firmer on my computer. And, seeing that commercial has nothing to do with my searching last week for quick ways to tone my stomach muscles or firm my thighs or have a sexier butt. Nothing at all. The two are unrelated.

I purchased the Abmaster and Ski-Glider and even unboxed them. They're in my exercise room waiting for me to finish my ice cream. I don't understand why I don't have the physique or fitness I desire. Maybe there's better exercise equipment that will get me where I tell myself I want to go while eating ice cream every night. There has to be.

It is much more satisfying to think that my wife or husband or lover or kids will love me more after I vigorously express my anger. Sometimes shouting and threatening has that effect.

I pout and sulk when my co-workers hurt my feelings hoping that my pout will make them see it my way. I want my pout to make them like me more, agree with me more. Of course, I don't pout at or yell at my boss or my customers. I'm not stupid! They'd take it the wrong way.

It is also safer to ignore any implications of collective result. We can't explain why a large number of kids are alienated and depressed, or why the youngest among us have the highest rates of prescribed anti-anxiety medication use. It has nothing to do with not having a sustained parental presence in the home. Neither does it have anything to do with allowing our children to be bombarded with unrealistic messages about how they should look, when they should have sex for the first time, or whether drug use is pleasurable. They text rather than talk to us at the dinner table and we don't feel up to the struggle of making the demand for connection. Their alienation has nothing to do with our actions or lack of action.

Why did so many UK and American citizens vote against their obvious best interests? In the first instance, the UK voters cut themselves off from the benefit of associating with the wider European community. In the second instance, the US voters elected a dangerously unqualified president. These votes had nothing to do with the latent racism within both cultures, or the spreading distance between the privileged 1% and the vast majority of the people, or with media pandering. No one can explain it really. It just happened. Let's hope it's over soon.

The apparent clash of civilizations between the West, Islamic Cultures, and Asia has nothing to do with historical causes. Today's current strain between the West and Islam has nothing to do with the Crusades. Or with the Islamic invasions of Palestine and North Africa in the 7th century. Or with the post-World War 1 peace that carved up the Middle East without asking the opinion of the peoples who lived there. It has nothing to do with vast inequality in terms of health, wealth, or freedom. The Islamic world is just angry at us and we don't know why they appear to hate us. It doesn't have an identifiable cause.

Let's ignore the growing collision between China and the West. China's growing youthful population and driven pursuit of economic leadership aren't a threat. The West will always be ahead. Why should we be afraid if China corners the world market on the rare metals needed to make our computers, satellites, phones, and more? Our past treatment of the Chinese as inferior will have no impact on how they treat us in the near future. None.

A third dangerous truth to be understood upon awakening is the link between cause and effect in our world.

Plant corn, get corn. That's the law of karma. The word "karma" means action and points at this relationship. If you plant corn you never get watermelon. Unless someone snuck a watermelon seed into your corn seeds. Or maybe in today's

world a genetically modified corn seed with watermelon genes. When you plant corn, you get corn.

One long-standing bit of wisdom is that if we want to understand what's happening now, look at what went before. If we want to understand what's coming next, look at what we are doing now. Of course, we live in a complex world and there isn't a simple "single cause to single effect" link. There's no guarantee that Hitler didn't have a happy rebirth. But there is a certainty that Hitler's fear and craziness, and his sociopathic leadership helped give rise to a global conflict that took millions upon millions of lives and changed the world forever. Plant race hatred; get a world stained by race hatred.

Buddha is said to have taught, "Hatred never ceases by hatred, but by love alone is healed. This is an ancient and eternal law." Understanding result or karma does NOT mean that effects can't be changed. Seventy years of dedicated effort after the conflagration of the Second World War lead us

36

to a united and prosperous Europe where Germany, England, and France cooperate for the common good. But seventy years of hard effort can be undone with a short, concerted focus on planting hatred and division once again. It's not certain what effect Brexit, Britain's exit from the European Union, will have on Europe's overall happiness. However, one thing is certain, when you plant division, you get division.

Understanding result allows us to have a realistic view of how to create a future. Most of us have God or Gods that we pray to. We ask these Gods for help, for intervention, or to change our future. The wise among the faithful then roll up their shirt sleeves and get to work. As one wise man once told me, "God shows up and blesses after you've done the hard work of digging and planting." Then to my surprise, he added, "God doesn't guarantee the rain, so work hard and keep an open eye on the skies. Irrigate if you need to." We were talking about how to make spiritual progress, not gardening, but I knew what he meant.

If you want to live in a world that values the truth, don't lie. Lies create a world of deception. If you wish to live in a world of prosperity, don't hoard. Hoarding creates a poverty of mind and heart, where you feel needy, even when you're surrounded by riches. Instead of hoarding, practice generosity. Being generous makes you feel rich and it helps everyone. If you wish to be happy, be grateful and think of others. Don't think of your own happiness. Chasing happiness only creates the desire for the next thrill, the next pleasure, the next whatever. Gratitude opens your heart and thinking of others fills your heart with love. Together, gratitude and thinking of others create the conditions that plant happiness to grow happiness.

If taking responsibility for how things turn out threatens you, if you'd rather leave it all in the hands of God, or luck, or happenstance, then waking up to the truth of result is dangerous. Avoid connecting your actions with the world you live in as much as possible. If nothing else works, blame God.

Me

If you want to stay happy, hold onto your idea of "me." You know, that "me" we each think we are. When you look out through your eyes it certainly feels like the entire world is centered around you. It's felt that way for as long as you can remember. And it's not only you. Everyone feels this way, as if they are the center of the universe. What could be wrong with that?

Never admit, especially to yourself, that "me" is a story you've been telling yourself for as long as you can remember. Think back to your earliest memories, whether happy or sad. That's when you became conscious of "me." You were "me" before that but you just don't remember. From those earliest memories you have a story. One memory is your story of your first day at school. Another memory may be the story of a childhood bully or best pal. A third memory may be the story of your first kiss, winning a contest, or failing a test at school.

On and on, since that first memory, you've been building the story. Since you've worked on it for a long time now, wouldn't it be a shame to let it go? Who would you be if you let your story go? You might not remember who to love and who to be angry with. You might forget you prefer chocolate over vanilla, forget that you take soy milk in your latte, or that you like to dance. How would you remember without telling yourself the story over and over again?

The so called fact that you are no longer the four year-old playing in the grass with your brother, which was my first memory, isn't important. Of course I'm that same person and you are the same person who experienced your first memory. Your loves and disappointments and accomplishments haven't changed you a bit. OK, maybe you have added some good things and you have a few dents and bruises, but you're still "me."

Don't listen if some trickster meditator asks you to find "me." It doesn't matter if you've had dental implants, cataract lens replacements, or that you're now bald. Nothing changes. We are still the same "me." Your sense of "me" doesn't have to live anywhere in the body or be identifiable as this or that. My sense of "me" isn't in my teeth or else my dental implants would change me. "Me" isn't in the lenses of my eyes or else that lens replacement surgery would change me. Even if I had a heart transplant I would still be "me!" Wouldn't I? Why should "me" have to be like everything else we say is real? You know you're a "me" and so do I, so keep that story going.

My sense of "me" isn't in my thoughts or my emotions or my preference for chocolate over vanilla. Different thoughts are all just part of the experience of "me." Emotions can change like the weather. So what? "Me" holds the stories of all my thoughts and loves and hates and indifferences for as long as I can remember. The fact that they are all steadily changing can't mean they're not the same "me" I've always been.

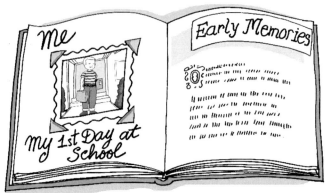

Book Of Me

A fourth dangerous truth to be understood upon awakening is that "Me" is a construct, a story we tell ourselves to make ourselves feel OK.

Each of us experiences the world as if the world were centered around us. That's how our senses work. It feels as if something central and within is looking out, listening, touching, smelling, tasting. When our awareness looks within, it feels as if this ongoing stream of experience has a central experiencer. We call this feeling "me." Each of us forgets that this "me" is something we made up to make sense of the stream of experience, to organize *things so we can survive and thrive. "Me" is like the wizard in the story of the Wizard of Oz. In the story of Oz, there's really no one behind the curtain other than a small man speaking through a large megaphone. The wizard's voice sounds large and convincing. Everyone has forgotten that there's really no wizard there.*

Having a sense of "me" serves a good purpose. It allows us to make sense of life and to grow and be alive. Real problems with "me" only happen when we either forget that we've made it up or when we take it too seriously. When either of those happens, you might get stuck hating something "me" decided had hurt "me" so many years ago. So much of the conflict in our world is linked to remembered slights and wrongs that are long past.

We get so busy fighting old conflicts that we can forget to look at today's problems like climate change, or drought, or famine, or the refugee crisis. So today, many of us ignore the melting polar ice caps and disappearing permafrost to focus on

religious issues older than the Crusades of the 11th
century.

On a more personal level, we might remain in a relationship when we are no longer loved because "me" is married to you. Even more sadly, "me" might miss when love arrives because "me" is stuck in old resentments. Whether our sense of "me" is a help or a curse completely depends on whether we remember that we made "me" up.

If you want to live in a world that values "me" then don't wake up to your made-up "me". Instead, keep your story going. Don't admit to any essential changes in who your "me" is. You've always been "me." You may grow and even change but this essential, unfindable, undefinable "me" is real. Stick with the story and you'll stay happy.

Don't meditate. Meditation will eventually point out the temporary nature of your "me." Meditation will show you how "me" is constantly shifting and changing. Of course, you can meditate to calm "me" down and find your groove. But remember, it's dangerous to your happiness. Maybe it would be better to have an ice cream cone or take something that helps "me" be happy.

Openness

An important key to maintaining our sense of safety and security is to maintain our sense of a closed reality. This means things are exactly what we think they are. It is more comforting, easier to understand, generally matches our dreams and illusions, and it is way better to think things are real.

For example, the computer that I am using to write this book is and will remain a computer. It was once shiny and the newest model when I took it out of the box. Now it is slightly older and there are newer models. My last computer broke when the screen cracked. Even though it had all the same parts and functioned much the same as it did the day before the screen cracked, somehow its computer-ness left and it became a useless piece of techno-junk.

Everything more or less follows this same pattern. We see the entire pyramid and not the building blocks that contribute to make the pyramid. Would there be pyramids without these stones?

Does the idea of pyramids exist somewhere, maybe out in space, without any stones? How about the chair you are sitting on? Perhaps your chair has legs and arms and a back. It certainly has a seat. When all these pieces of chair were lying around the furniture factory, waiting to be assembled into your chair, chair-ness must have been laying around also. The unassembled pieces aren't a chair. When all the pieces are put together somehow chair happens. Why isn't this explained in my Ikea assembly instructions?

This closed-system, real way of looking at things, is how we experience our bodies. How often do we contemplate our spleen, gall bladder, or left ventricle? We don't think about the component parts of our blood let alone the building blocks of hemoglobin, various blood proteins, and blood stuff. We think even less about the chromosomes that cause all this blood stuff to happen. We think least of all about the neutrons, protons, electrons, quarks and other subatomic bits and pieces that build the chromosomes which key the building of the blood stuff that circulates through the left ventricle of our hearts and that make up this thing we call our body.

Our most cherished relationships also benefit from this closed way of looking at them. Your lover will always be your lover. Your relationship doesn't have any parts even if there are two of you. More importantly, your love relationship doesn't need any maintenance or new energy because it has that always and forever love thing. Don't think about previous lovers or lost friendships. They must not have been the real thing like this love. There is no beginning, middle, or end to your love story. You don't need to change anything even if your lover could do better on that one little thing that annoys you, like the thing with the toilet seat. The same benefit of having a reliable and constant understanding of your lover applies to your friends, colleagues, neighbors, enemies, everyone. They will always stay who you think they are.

Of course, everything slowly falls apart. This is one of the fundamental insights of how we understand the universe. It's even called a law in Physics, the Law of Entropy. Pyramids are worn away by sand and wind and slowly fade back into the desert. Old chairs get chipped and worn and maybe even break as the glue that holds the legs and arms and seat together dries out and becomes brittle. One day, you rest a heavy bag of groceries on the chair and the old chair falls apart. Where did chair go in that pile of wood and groceries on your floor?

Ignore this understanding that everything is made out of other, smaller parts and things. Ignore that everything wears out eventually. Even the stars will fade. Things are what they seem to be. They have always been that way and will stay that way.

A fifth dangerous truth to be understood upon awakening is that reality itself is a made-up-idea that creates a closed or stable sense of predictability from the constantly changing and unpredictable flow of life. We make up this story of reality to help us feel safe and to allow us to work with the flow of life.

Everything we can observe started sometime, hangs out for a while, and then fades away. We can look forever and not find any permanent phenomena. Even the longest-lived phenomena, like stars, eventually transform. They explode as nova, maybe even collapse and become black holes. The earth will pass away. It began sometime very long ago and will not be here anymore sometime in the distant future. Nailing down Earth's time span is just a discussion of details.

Not only do things appear and then fade away, everything that does appear seems to be made of smaller and smaller parts. Chairs have legs and arms and seats. The wood of those legs and arms and seats have molecules that are made of atoms that are made of tinier parts. When examined under the most powerful of microscopes, most of what makes up the so-called atom is the space between its parts. There's more space than stuff in most things.

Part of our human genius has been to assemble things and turn them into something else, like the chair parts assembled into a chair. We give these new things a name to point at the new thing that happens when the parts all come together. Part of our human craziness is that after giving this new thing a name, we trick ourselves into forgetting that we made the name up. We act as if the new-named-thing is real and has always been there. This forgetting trick creates a closed system where we regard reality as the same thing as the names and opinions we have about all the different things we experience.

One important benefit of adopting the open system point of view is that things and people are allowed to change. A very important side effect of this open system point of view is that, because everything can change, we are more responsible for how we experience our world.

If you want to live in a world that has a strong sense of permanent reality, a world that is a closed system, then don't wake up. It will challenge your sense of what is real and push you to take more responsibility. Who wants more responsibility? I don't. I want a predictable world where the things I like are always good, the same predictable good everywhere, like McDonald's hamburgers. Billions served and all the same, yum!

I also want a predictable world that conforms to my expectations. My enemies will always be my enemies. My friends will always be my friends. No one has changed since I graduated high school, maybe even before. My favorite chair will always be the same favorite chair. I can ignore that everything is made up of parts, that everything has a beginning, middle, and an end. Why complicate things with understanding how it all works. My take on a closed reality works just fine.

Awake Mind

If you want to stay asleep, to continue enjoying your dreams, then do everything you can to avoid waking up your mind. You know what your thoughts and memories are. They are right. Your thoughts completely and accurately reflect reality. Your memory is accurate and beyond question. Thinking about your mind like it was a computer is a useful metaphor even though your mind is not actually like a computer and nothing is hardwired there or stored as electrical charges in the same way computer data is.

Your mind is a thing. It holds thoughts and memories like data. You think about something and find it in your mind. You search your memories and find a totally accurate reflection of what happened. These thoughts and memories are available to you, just like the data on your computer is available to you whenever you want. When you don't want a memory, it just goes back to the data bank and stays there. To use an even older metaphor, your memory waits, like a library book waiting on a shelf, for you to reopen it sometime in the future. Your memory, like a library book always stays the same. Recalling and repeating the memory has no effect on it.

Change only happens when new and better information is added. It's like an upgrade to my computer's operating system or a new edition of a familiar book in the library. Change in my mind, my thoughts, my opinions, or my memory is never about things being different than they were before. To use a familiar example, I've always preferred the intensity of chocolate to other flavors of ice cream. My brief dalliance with the subtlety of lemon sorbet was a mistake that I soon corrected. Chocolate is my favorite. Just as my ice cream flavor has not changed, neither have my thoughts about life, my political opinions, or my childhood memories.

It's not important that no one has ever been able to define or adequately explain mind. No one I know denies having a mind. That should be good enough. Why worry that this experience called mind appears to constantly change like the weather? Is it important that sometimes my thoughts are peaceful and then at other times I fly off into a rant or rage? Why should what happens with my senses have any important effect on mind. Twelve hours of playing *Grand Theft Auto* or *Call of Duty: Infinite Warfare* has nothing to do with my feeling simultaneously drained of energy and ready to rage. My mind and my senses have nothing to do with each other. Mind is its own thing and that thing is at the essence of me.

A sixth, dangerous truth to be understood upon awakening is that having a mind is more of an act than a thing. In fact Mind is not a thing. It is an open, dynamic process.

One of the dangers of practicing meditation is that we begin to notice that our thoughts, memories, and emotions are constantly changing. One part of meditating is to become aware of this *process. We notice that a thought about when meditation will be over and we can have lunch, seemingly from nowhere. This waiting-for-lunch-thought hangs out for a while and then is replaced by the thought of what we will have for lunch. The menu thought is then replaced by our memory of being disappointed by what we had for breakfast. This process of thoughts flows endlessly by as we meditate and observe. It is like an unending river. We sit and watch the waters of thought, memory, emotion, and sensation flow by. The waters are constantly changing but we always just call them river. Equally we call the flow of thought-memory-emotion-sensation mind.*

A second dangerous insight that comes from meditating is that we might begin to think about water pollution in the river of our thoughts, feelings, opinions and sensation. Mind doesn't just float away. It continues to flow past us like a river that moves in a great circle. Whatever we throw into our minds eventually flows past again in one form or another. If our mind at all resembles a computer, then this acronym from the earliest days of modern programming applies: GIGO. Garbage in, garbage out. When we practice thinking thoughts of hatred and anger, our mind grows constantly more angry. If we practice being calm and kind, peace grows in our mind.

The most dangerous insight that comes from meditating is that we might notice that there is brightness to being awake. We have the capability to know, to sense, to remember, to dream. This bright capability is all around, beneath, beyond the mere content of our thoughts. We might begin to think that having a mind is more about this capability than it is about the ever changing content of our thoughts, memories, and opinions.

If you want to keep it simple and be at ease, if you don't want to have to take responsibility for your mind or have a sharper understanding of what mind is, avoid waking up. Do not meditate. Meditation is somewhat like system maintenance on your personal hard-drive. Paying attention to how your senses impact mind is too much work. Noticing that every thought you ever had before this one has disappeared, well that's simply depressing. It is much better to just think of mind as a computer with the best possible programs. You can upgrade when you want to. There is never a need to wake up, clean the cache, delete duplicate or outdated programs, or remove cookies. Everything is fine. Never change your password. Just click on unearned wealth + happiness and everything will be perfect.

Open Heart

You definitely don't want to experience open heartedness. You would feel everything, both pain and pleasure, both heartbreak and love. You'd remember the bad times as well as the good. You'd feel both anxiety and excitement. Open hearts are very messy. Yuck!

It's way better to have a well-managed heart. I know when to open the door to my heart and when to keep your heart's door closed. I keep it closed most of the time. It's safer that way.

If you opened your heart to your family, things would get emotionally really messy. Your husband or wife, or lover can have so many needs. An open heart would require you to be aware of those needs. It's so much easier to pigeonhole your husband, wife, or lover into their familiar category. "You know Bob; he's always sad and low energy." And, "You know Sally, she's been angry forever." And, "We've said it all to each other so many times already. We don't talk much anymore except about the kids." If you've been together for so many years, you know who the other person is. There are no surprises this way. You have the same familiar distance and comfort level every day, every week, every month, every year on into decades of life together.

You certainly don't want to open the door to your heart for your work-mates or for your neighbors. Keep your heart safely latched. When your boss' wife is diagnosed with cancer, don't let that touch your heart. Tell him you're sorry, ask what the doctors say to do, spend up to five minutes listening and appear to be sympathetic. Then steer the conversation back to work, to the project you're working on, or the task you were given to complete. It's much tidier that way. Your boss will think you care and that's really the point, isn't it? If you allowed yourself to really care, then you might worry about your own health or the health of your partner or parent.

Worry gets in the way of productivity. When your secretary tells you her child is sick or her father is in the hospital, look sympathetic. Ask how much time she needs to take care of her child or to be with her dad. If necessary, let her take an unscheduled vacation day. If it's unavoidable and if you're really feeling generous, let her have leave without pay. But don't let yourself feel any true resonance with her predicament. You need to avoid unexpected emergencies. You need to keep working to be safe.

Real feelings are threatening. Why would you want to open your heart to strangers? Your world is just fine without any new people. If you opened your heart to your family, things would get emotionally really messy.

No! An open heart just brings lots of demands to feel, to be real, to let life in. Don't go there.

IN CASE OF
EMERGENCY,
BREAK GLASS

A seventh, dangerous truth to be understood upon awakening is that having an Open Heart means we will feel everything. Having an Open Heart is a dangerous statement of hope and requires tremendous courage. Keeping our heart open requires work.

One of the dangers of waking up is that we increasingly feel more. Because we know that things are just a story, we can add new chapters or edit old ones. We aren't stuck. This helps unstick our heart. When we recognized how everything is impermanent, we gained the recognition that all feelings and emotions are equally impermanent. No bad day has to last forever. No grudge has to be held till we die. And sadly, even when love is true till death do you part; death is inevitable. That's just how life is.

Because we recognize the pattern of result, we become aware that what we put into our heart affects what we feel. Rehearse memories of hate then we will feel more hate. Practice being grateful and we suddenly find ourselves more satisfied and surprisingly generous. Look for moments of love and we feel a sweet swelling of the heart. Because we have practiced openness, we are available for new experiences. This includes new feelings. Because our mind is awake, we know that there is a brightness within us that longs to experience, to know, and to love.

When we wake up, our heart increasingly becomes more like a well-tuned musical instrument, like a piano. When we play "C" on one piano string, all the other "C" strings resonate. They are in sympathy with each other. The awake heart is like this, sympathetic and resonant. The more we practice being awake, the more we will feel. When you are happy you'll feel fully happy. When your child is sad, you will resonate with that sadness. When your friends at work are stressed out, you will feel their stress.

The Open Heart feels more and more as it grows.

Avoid this if at all possible. Feelings are messy and demanding. They get in the way of getting things done. They require you to pause and consider, appreciate, resonate with life. You have work to do. The kids have to get to soccer camp. You haven't responded to today's emails yet. Your

Facebook, Instagram, Pinterest, Linked-In connections are waiting to hear from you. There's not really enough time for feeling. It's much better to keep your heart closed most of the time. You will have time to feel when you're on vacation or after you retire.

Showing Up

You absolutely don't want to show up for your life. If you show up, things will be expected of you. You'll be asked to help, to be present, to pitch in. Your family, friends, and neighbors will wonder what's going on with you, what you're feeling, and what you are up to. They'll want an open window into who you are. Your workmates will expect you to be available and to perform. Work will be about much more than your last performance evaluation or your attendance record. Why allow yourself to be visible?

Have you ever noticed that most people, sitting in their air-conditioned cars, behind closed windows, act as if they're invisible? Sometimes you can catch them being themselves. Talking to themselves. Singing aloud and chair dancing to the radio. Having an argument with themselves. Picking their nose. Looking sad or something else. For a brief moment, when you look through their car window, you can see them. But when they become aware that you're looking, these car people suddenly become someone else. They become normal. No talking, singing, dancing, nose picking, sadness or anything else; just normal. Boring.

The predictable, safe, sane life is just like those car people after you've seen them. It is boring and normal. You don't have to be really present. You just can't be marked down as absent. So you are sort of in your marriage. You say "Good morning" and "I love you" but the excitement is gone.

You love your kids and hope they do exactly what you'd do. They feel just what you'd feel, of course. Your neighbors are OK. They put out their trash on garbage day and keep their lawns tidy. You say "Hello" over the fence. Why would you need to know that your neighbors' favorite aunt died yesterday? You'd have to send flowers, maybe even go to the funeral. It's better to keep it simple.

You watch the same movies as everyone else, read the same books, pray to the same God, more or less. You are having a sweet dream of a life, a little excitement but not too much. You had some passion when you were younger, but now you've settled down. You'll be able to pay off your mortgage and retire, if nothing really bad happens. This is as good as you can expect, isn't it?

The eighth and most dangerous truth to be understood upon awakening is that awakened life demands that we show up. It will no longer be enough for us to just not be counted absent. Feeling more and recognizing the open flow of life, we will experience the demand to be present and to let life touch us. We will be expected to help.

Waking up is being 100% alive. When you awaken your senses, your heart is available, and you begin to notice everyone and everything around you. You notice the look of expectation in your partner's eyes. You hear the hope for connection in your children's voices when they ask for your help with a chore. You feel the loneliness and longing of your neighbor when she tells you about her aunt's death. You resonate with the tiredness of your workmates as you push to finish a project on time. You see, hear, taste, touch, smell, and feel it all. Your mind is awake and active and you are present.

Being truly present means that not only do we see the world but the world can touch us. This is the real meaning of vulnerable. The world can get at us. And it will. The garden asks to be weeded. The house needs to be painted. That dripping faucet would appreciate attention. And our partner, our family, our neighbors and everyone else want a slice of us.

Showing up and being open is a challenge. No one can be everything that everyone wants. That would be overwhelming. We have to somehow manage showing up without drowning in demands.

72

That might look like being present where and when we can without trying to save the entire world.

You won't take away the world's sadness but you can listen to your neighbor tell you about her aunt. You can't prevent sickness and death. No one can. But you can let yourself feel and resonate with your secretary's worries about a sick father. You might not change the world but you could coach your daughter's soccer team. You could shovel your aged neighbor's walk when it snows. You could look the cashier at the supermarket in the eye and say "Hello" as she bags your groceries. You can show up.

Each time we show up, we build a little more capacity to just be the persons we are, and to not pretend to be invisible like those car people.

Because showing up is demanding, you really want to avoid this result. Staying safely asleep within your dream world is so much less scary, so much better. No one can really see you as long as the windows are rolled up. Your presence doesn't really matter anyway. What good can one person do? You can't affect any meaningful changes. If everyone just keeps looking straight ahead, and not making demands, you'll get through life. Nothing bad will happen.

Then you die.

I certainly don't want to look like uncle Harry did. The funeral home did a horrible job with him. He looked really bad. I hope that I'm a good-looking corpse when my time comes.

Strategies For Staying Asleep

The following list is only a beginning. It's up to you to identify those activities and ways of being that threaten your peaceful, dream filled sleep.

- **Avoid Meditation.**

  This is the most dangerous activity can undertake if you wish to stay asleep. Meditation is designed to wake you up. If you have to, buy a meditation cushion and allow your friends to be impressed, but don't practice. If you are forced to meditate, pretend that you are following whatever instructions you receive but really just continue to follow the fantasies and thoughts in your head.

- **Don't read anything with new or challenging ideas.**

  Books can be very dangerous too. They contain new thoughts and can question your cherished assumptions about life. Don't read anything like this. Perhaps it would be best to avoid reading anything longer than 100 words in length. That way you can be confident that you will avoid serious challenges.

- **Watch lots of movies and TV shows on your choice of streaming video platform.**

  Video streaming services are filled with diverting, sexy, compelling tales where heroes always win, where you can escape zombies, fight aliens, find new loves, and more. Spy movies, cop movies, lawyer movies, and scary movies: they all allow you to feel like you're doing something while you aren't really doing anything at all. It's like being asleep even while you're awake and you can eat popcorn while you continue to dream.

- **Watch lots of YouTube videos of cats and other people having fun.**
  Videos of other people having adventures, doing fun things, or laughing at their pets is a great substitute for the messiness of having your own adventure, fun, or pet. You get all the enjoyment without the commitment plus you can share them with your friends on Facebook.

- **Don't read or view any in-depth news coverage about anything.**
  Understanding what is really going on in your world is a chore. Restrict your news consumption to the easily digested

slogan or headline level discussions. Anything else risks your assumptions and begins a slippery slide into asking questions.

- **Stay home.**
  Enough said. Home is comfortable, like a cocoon. There's frozen pizza and beer in the fridge.

- **Sleep a lot.**
  This saves energy and is very conducive to staying secure in your dreams.

- **Eat junk food.**
  A healthy diet generates physical energy that will make you want to do things. A diet of processed foods, that's low in fiber and high in sugar and refined starches, will help you stay asleep.

- **Value fantasy over doing.**
  It is way easier to think about learning to play a musical instrument, or about

taking a trip to somewhere new or about learning a new skill at work than it is to do any of these things. It is much easier to fantasize about finding happiness and satisfaction in a perfect relationship than to go about the messy business of meeting people, dating, getting to know someone, and the rest. Keep it simple. Keep it easy. Avoid the wear and tear of doing anything. Just develop your fantasy muscle.

- **Avoid responsibility at home, at work, and in your community.**
When you take responsibility you will be expected to show up. Because showing up is so dangerous compared to staying asleep, avoid all the responsibility you can. Let someone else shoulder the task of doing what is needed. Someone else can do the dishes at home. A colleague can volunteer to stay late to help that customer. Your neighbors can volunteer to maintain that community garden, or to

be crossing guards for the kids, or to be volunteer firefighters. If you don't volunteer someone else will do it and you can stay asleep.

Afterword

Though this book may read like a defense of staying asleep and remaining confused about life, it is not a defense of either. **My wish for this book is that it will serve as a very gentle alarm bell, penetrating sleep with humor and reminding you of the possibility of awakening***.*

Almost everyone alive experiences life like a dream. We find ourselves born into the story of a family, a community, a nation, and a religion. We generally don't feel that we have permission to question these stories. Our universal story is that we are independent "selves," little universes of solitary experience. We call this experience "me" and dedicate almost all of our life's energy to making a better "me" story.

Very few individuals allow themselves the wisdom of waking up to how interconnected we all are. Each individual is just a part of an amazingly complex and interconnected web of experience.

For example, we would not be alive if our digestive tract wasn't home to billions, maybe even trillions of bacteria. Each of these bacteria is alive and somewhat independent, just like us. Their unseen and unnoticed life processes keep you alive. Each of us plays host to billions of other sensing, feeling beings that are invisible to us. Yet, we keep thinking we are just one thing, one person.

We lull ourselves to sleep even further by entertaining the dream that there is some undefined "me" or "self" inside that owns our thoughts and feelings. This is how it seems when we are lost in the dream. But who is this someone who owns my thoughts, feelings, and experiences?

No one has ever been able to say. No one has ever found the true self that convinces everyone else. The self is not like gravity, a demonstrable law of nature. Nor is the self like the sunrise. When the skies are clear, anyone with vision can tell when the sun has risen above the horizon. The self is more like a story we tell. Telling helps us make sense of the world. Awakening reminds us that "me" is a story.

Many meditators say they want to awaken while clinging to the dream that lulls them to sleep. Our meditation cushions gather dust in a corner. When we do meditate, nothing seems to change.

I offer this short book with hope that we can look at what keeps us from awakening. We can recognize what keeps us from opening our minds and hearts and being present. If we clearly identify what choices, desires, and assumptions keep us asleep, then we can choose to wake up or choose to enjoy our dreams for as long as they last.